CN01460714

Wroughton and Where to Find them

and

Where to Find them

By
Joy McNally-Bells

Front cover photograph shows Sarah Page and her family taken just before her son Archie, standing centre, age 18, is sent to France in 1917. Mildred age 15 stands on the left and Agnes age 12 sits in front of her. Reginald age 10 sits on the floor. The family lived at number 4 Brimble Hill, Wroughton

Dedication

To Robin, who inspires my curiosity and to all those who have experienced the paranormal and shared their stories with me.

Preface

I originally created this ghost walk to get my own children out of the house for some exercise and fresh air when they were young. At that time I only knew three or four ghost stories about Wroughton, mostly heard from my mother and grandfather who were both born in the village. (My mother in 1923 and my grandfather in 1899). As time has gone on however and people have learnt about my fascination for ghosts I've been approached on many an occasion with a whispered 'I've got a ghost story. Would you like to hear it?'

This is how I've gathered many more stories, some utterly bizarre like the coloured dancing orbs in the High Street others more traditional like the woman in white that haunts the graveyard. I've tried to research each tale. Sometimes there's some historical evidence which might explain a ghostly presence, sometimes I've been told the same story by two different people who aren't aware of each other's ghostly experience and therefore reinforce the creepy tale…and sometimes there's nothing to give even an inkling as to why a ghost is haunting a village location - but it does.

If you've had a supernatural experience associated with a place in Wroughton that you would be happy for me to add to these ghost stories I would love to hear it. Eventually I want to print a comprehensive guide to the ghosts of Wroughton and include a street map of ghostly sightings, but that is for another day. The stories included in this book are the ghostly tales and myths that occur as one walks from St John the Baptist and St Helen's Church at the top of Church Hill down the High Street to the Brown Jack public house.

I would like to thank everyone who has shared a ghostly story, local myth or odd experience. My gratitude goes to Alexandra Moulding, Rosemary Allen, Richard Clarke, Sharon Smith, Tracie Lea, Amanda Davey, Nicky Wooff, the landlords and landladies of some of Wroughton's public houses and many more who've asked me not to give their names and others I don't even know.

As well as ghosts I've also spent time looking at local legends and the word of mouth stories that have come down through the generations. I've explored the history that might account for certain tales and have tried to sprinkle the walk with snippets of historical fact to flesh the bones of these ghostly stories. For this I am indebted to the work of Wroughton History Group for the thorough historical research they have undertaken and produced in their fabulous Wroughton History books. I've also found interesting information in the work of the great Swindon poet Alfred Williams whose descriptions of Wroughton in the early 1900's are compassionate and illuminating. The extremely comprehensive website British History Online has also been a very helpful reference.

I must also give an immense debt of gratitude to Danny Hicks who has helped with editing and allowed me to use many photographs stored in the Wroughton History Group archive.

This is an offering which I hope excites your curiosity; a collection of ghost stories and myths from the village of Wroughton, specific to Church Hill, The High Street and Priors Hill. It is not a perfectly executed grammatical presentation of highly edited fictions.

So when the nights begin to draw in and you catch a glimpse of something inexplicable in your periphery vision or hear a strange cry carried on the wind, maybe you'll ask the same question my son asked all those years ago... 'Is it time for a ghost walk?'

Joy McNally-Bells

31/10/2019

Is Wroughton the most haunted village in England?
A little background history

I'm always amazed that there are so many ghost stories associated with our village. Some are generic and are probably told in one form or another all over the country, while others are specific to Wroughton. So I thought I'd begin with a little background history of Wroughton. After all where do ghosts come from if not the past? (Although even this is open to debate). If you're not interested in the history please feel free to skip to the next chapter. Be aware however that the history of Wroughton provides context for many of our ghostly stories and is often referred to.

Old Wroughton was originally known as Ellendun, and that name can still be heard in daily use e.g. The Ellendune Hall, The Ellendune Shopping Centre and at some time the houses at the Swindon end of Perry's Lane were called Ellendune Houses. Blue name plates from the 1920's are still attached to the end houses proclaiming 'Ellendune Houses'.

Ellendune is mentioned over a century before the Norman Conquest in the Anglo Saxon Charter of 956. Here it describes a church wall in the boundary of Ellendun. The name goes back even further to 890, where the Anglo Saxon Chronicles outline the boundary of Ellendun. A description of the boundary includes the Ridgeway, which still comprises part of the boundary of Wroughton today.

Ellendune can be traced back even further to the year 825. In September of that year a great battle was fought between the people of Wessex led by King Egbert and the Mercians let by Beornwulf. This battle has been described as 'one of the most decisive battles of Anglo-Saxon history'. One suggested place of the battle is on the downs above Markham bottom.

It can be assumed with relative confidence that the name Ellendune has been associated with the village for 1200 years or more.

Going forward in time, Ellendune became known as Wroughton sometime in the 15th Century which is a reference to the River Worf. The River Worf is in turn an old name for the River Ray, which is the stream we see running through Wroughton today.

Historically the Parish of Wroughton has evidenced peoples from every era, from pre-history to modern times. Local Museums abound with arrows and spear heads, pottery and coins. There are also many legends, from Cromwell stabling his horses at the Fox and Hounds during the English Civil War to Queen Elizabeth I getting a crick in her neck when the wind shot through her carriage going down Brimble Hill. Hence the name of the house on the bend, Windshot House.

Our village has been the home of many generations of villagers before us. The ghosts of our village's past are everywhere, from the names of our streets to the names on the graves in our church yard.
But the question remains
…are the ghosts of Wroughton's past still with us?

Map of the village of Wroughton

It begins with a name…

There are several suggestions as to where the name Ellendune originally came from. Alder Tree Down suggests that many alder trees grew here, whilst another possibility is that Ella was the name of a local clan chief and this was his village or fort so, - Ella's down. The story that I like best and which has a sense of our pre Christian forebears is that it is named after the pagan Goddess Ellen, who has antlers like the pagan God Herne, she is known as the Goddess of the ways. This is interesting given our close proximity to the ancient Ridgeway which is surely a description of 'the ways' of ancient time. She also has strong links to the fairy folk, though I haven't been told any fairy stories associated with Wroughton…yet.

Other evidence linking the Goddess Ellen to Wroughton is the interchangeability of the name Ellen with Helen. As far back as 956 Helen's Thorn was recorded as a landmark on the boundary between the manors of Elcombe and Ellendune and another fact supporting the theory that Ellen was once a pagan Goddess worshipped in this area is the dual dedication of the old church. It is dedicated to St John the Baptist and St Helen. Could the St Helen in this dedication refer to Ellen and actually have been added to the dedication as a way of supplanting pre Christian beliefs? Known as Ellendune Church up until the 19th Century, who's to know what ancient rural superstitions were overcome by including Helen in this dedication.

If you know of any other OS map names or ancient buildings in the vicinity with Ellen or Helen assigned to them I'd love to hear about them.

Wroughton Parish Church dedicated to St John the Baptist and St Helen. Circa 1914

The ancient yew tree

As you walk down the path towards the large, wooden double doors of the church of St John the Baptist and St Helen, on your left you cannot fail to see a yew tree that is two or three hundred years old, maybe more. It may have been planted on purpose or seeded by the many yews that filled the churchyard over time by stint of the necessity for yew in the making of long bows. Or maybe its ancestor was an ancient yew where the druids once worshipped the Goddess Ellen.

Yew trees are known as the tree of the dead. It was believed that their roots dug into the surrounding graves and were nourished by the bodies of the dead. They are also believed to have great longevity, often being much older than they look.

When I was a child the boughs of the yew in Wroughton graveyard spread wide and heavy and hid many gravestones, however these days it has been sensibly pruned and looks a picture of health. Anyone who has been brought up in Wroughton or lived here for any length of time will know there is a ghostly legend associated with this ancient grave yard yew. The story tells that if you walk around the tree ten times with your eyes shut, when you stop and open them you will see a ghost. Another story says you must stick a pin in the tree before you begin your ten circuits of the trunk. I have tried both methods and been disappointed but it is something you may like to try yourself one day...

So, who is this ghost? Several different ghostly phenomenon have apparently been sighted. One of the ghosts is thought to be a clergy man. His tall figure is dressed in black and he wears a wig. Could this be the remorseful, sporting parson who preferred to go a hunting rather than conduct a funeral or a wedding? According to the Swindon poet Alfred Williams, corpses would be left in the church porch all night and mourners were sent home and would come back the next day in the hope that the parson would have returned from hunting.

Another ghostly phenomenon supposedly haunting the yew tree is a figure that hangs in the branches of the tree. The terrifying sight is supposed to be accompanied by the sound of the creaking rope by which he hangs.

Another story is that you may glimpse the sad figure of a woman in white who stands by the stone cross base, which is a monument you can see on the other side of the path to the yew tree. Long ago couples would be married at this stone, not in the church. Was the woman jilted? Did she meet an unhappy end? Is she stuck in this place?

Of course, if you walk around the tree 10 times with your eyes shut, not only might you fall over, you might be inclined to see anything formed by shadows as you open your eyes. That would simply be your imagination.

I was told by a Wroughton woman that early one hot, summer morning white mist was seen emanating from the yew tree. This led me to an interesting fact and might explain why the yew tree was revered in pagan times for its magical powers and also why more recently people have believed that they've seen a ghost here. I found out that on hot days yew trees release a gas called taxine which has the ability to cause hallucinations. Maybe the story about sticking a pin in the bark before lapping the tree is a druidic folk memory that is something to do with releasing the hallucinogenic gas.

Was it this gas, released in the heat of summer that changed perceptions and ensured these ghostly myths endured? The white gas interpreted as an apparition and its hallucinogenic effect creating illusions in the mind? Is it the gas that has led to these ghostly stories or are there real ghosts associated with the yew tree?

Wroughton Parish Church. The ancient yew tree is on the left of the church between the gravestones

The Swindon poet Alfred Williams, who wrote down the memories of Wroughton people in the early 19th Century

The stable school below operated as a school from the mid 1700's.
It is located in the front garden of Ivery House

Legge House below, known as the Top School opened in 1867

The playing children

The graveyard of the old church of St John the Baptist and St Helen is surprisingly the location of the first National school in Wroughton. Anyone of a certain age who has lived in the village their whole life will know that Legge House, in the grounds of the graveyard was the school for many years (see picture on p.12). However there were private schools in the village prior to this time.

 In the Garden of the Old Rectory House, now called Ivery House is an old stable block which is just in front of the rectory house and easily visible from the track through the graveyard (see picture on p.12). This was one of the first schools. In 1749 Thomas Benet of Saltrop, a local benefactor gave £40 a year to be divided between a school master here and another at Broad Hinton for the education of children in reading, writing, arithmetic and of course let's not forget the fourth R. Religion!

The upstairs of the old stable block was for girls and the downstairs for boys. By 1867 however the school was totally dilapidated and it's for this reason that Legge House was built, apparently from the stone of an old chapel in Elcombe dedicated to St Mary. When this became overcrowded an Infant school was built in 1874, which you will now recognise as the Church Hall and that was eventually replaced by another new school in School Lane in 1929, bearing the wonderful stonework in the doorway of the hare and the tortoise.

Enough of the potted history, let's return to the churchyard and the ghosts of playing children. I've been told that it's in moments of quiet, when sat on one of the benches in the sun, maybe reading a book or just enjoying the ambiance, that the silence is broken by the sound of children playing on the other side of the graveyard. It is a totally ordinary, everyday sound and nothing seems out of place.

The people that I've spoken to who have experienced this have all thought there were actual, real children playing in the graveyard. It's only when the expectation of seeing the children is not met that curiosity compels the listener to explore and within seconds the playful sound of children abruptly ceases. As I've found on several of my ghost walks someone has come up to me afterwards and corroborated this story with their own experience.

Given that the graveyard was a playground for children for several hundred years, is it surprising that the imprint of their voices playing games still fills the air? Why not visit the graveyard one quiet day yourself. You too may hear the sounds of children playing.

The Churchyard circa 1925, just visible to the right is the path leading to Legge House playground

Wroughton House

Wroughton House is the old building, standing behind the high wall on your right as you walk down the lane toward the churchyard (see picture on p.17). It is a very old house. It was rebuilt in 1760 and a well can be found within the present house walls indicating that a much older, smaller house once stood there. It is owned by the Codrington family who were highly esteemed members of the community. William Wyndham Codrington who lived here in the 19th century was a bit of an adventurer but also sat as magistrate.

It is the attic area that I wish to bring to your attention. The first time I heard stories about the attic was from a builder who was working there in the late 1990's. He said that despite it being summer the temperature intermittently dipped to freezing which spooked some of the workers who then refused to work there.

By itself this could be explainable, draughts, cold spots, it is an old house after all. However when I began to investigate more I found out that during the 2nd World War soldiers were billeted in the attic rooms. They told similar stories but in addition said that their belongings were often moved around and again many refused to stay.

Over the years more and more stories about Wroughton House have been sent to me. Many involve workmen who have been frightened by what seem to be inexplicable happenings. One told me that he would leave his tools at the end of the day neatly ordered to start work the next day, but when he arrived the next morning they had been moved. You have to consider that maybe someone who knew the stories deliberately moved the tools to frighten him. After all practical jokes are part of the Camaraderie of a team of tradespeople. (You just have to watch DIY SOS to know what I mean).

However, the stories kept on coming. I received a message from a lady whose father had worked in the house back in the 1970's. She told me that her father had said there was a ladder going from the ground floor through a hatch to an upstairs bedroom as there were no stairs. One day the ladder started moving as if someone was climbing it but no one was visible. On another occasion, ironically, a spirit level also went missing and was never found.

Another old Wroughtonian, many years dead himself, would tell the tale of going into the attic rooms and finding things had been moved around. His most frightening experience was coming across an old lady in crinolines sat in a rocking chair. He high-tailed it out and was reluctant to ever go back.

We have to remember that all this is subjective, drops in temperature, things moving can all be explained in a variety of ways. However it made me wonder that if there is a ghost, who could it be? Who is it tidying up after the workmen? Who would be the person to keep a house spick and span? Who would live in the attic in times gone by? A maid?

This is what I discovered. In 1900 a 29 year old maid was found hanging in the outhouse. Her name was Ada Truscott. What's Ada's story? What made her end her life so tragically? Is Ada still there?

I delved a little deeper and discovered Ada on the 1891 census 9 years earlier living in Bristol. She is described as cook/domestic and is the only servant for a family consisting of a mother and father and four sons. The four sons are of a similar age to the 21 year old Ada and are all students of engineering and medicine. One can only imagine the drudgery of her work. We can only guess what prompted her untimely death 9 years later. Loneliness? Pregnancy? The question remains. Does Ada still live in the attic?

Another explanation may be the playfulness of child spirits. Objects being taken and moved to other rooms might be explained by the inquisitiveness of children. In previous centuries death was a regular visitor and in the church there is a heart-breaking memorial to William Codrington's family whose deaths occurred at sadly short intervals. William died in 1802, his oldest daughter Mary-Anne in 1804 aged almost 13, his second daughter in 1806 aged 14 and two children Robert and Caroline who died in infancy.

Wroughton House, long time home of the Codrington Family, Photo taken from the roof of the church

Ivery House

The front of Ivery House in recent times

An early photograph of the rear of Ivery House

The journey into the village of Wroughton

To the right of the drive as you leave the church yard is Ivery House (see pictures on p.18). It was once the old rectory. The date stone is 1727 and the vicar at that time was John Sadler (1716 – 55), but it is likely that this date stone reflects when the house was refurbished as the original house is Elizabethan.

You will see a large yew hedge that acts as a garden boundary. This hedge has always been called the Oliver Cromwell Hedge in folk memory, it is very old and has historical and mysterious links to other areas of the village. Of which I will tell you later.

From the church we walk down the lane towards Church Hill and begin the descent towards the village. Stopping at the bench and facing the road you will be looking at a row of houses opposite that fronts a collection of cottages known locally as 'The Castle'. A ribbon of a path winds around the back and overlooks Markham Banks. Originally this may have been a castle in the same way as Barbury, Bincknell and Liddington, - that is an Iron Age Hillfort, however locally it has been suggested as the site of a Roman fort. The field to the right of Legge House has turned up Roman pottery in the past, so this may be likely.

The reason that I ask you to note this area is because I will mention it again in a moment when you reach the comfort of the Fox and Hounds public house. Here I invite you to go and purchase your preferred beverage and sit in a quiet corner and read about the very place in which you sit.

The Curtis Family, once residents of The Fox and Hounds

*Here is a picture of Frederick John Curtis, his wife Amelia Curtis (nee Austin)
and their three sons, Frederick John Junior, Frank and Charles. Frederick John
senior is the son of Luke Curtis who you will read about shortly. Luke lived at
what is now The Fox and Hounds from 1851 until at least 1887*

The Fox and Hounds

My Great Granny Hale cooked for a short time at the previously mentioned, Ivery House in the 1920's and my grandfather would sometimes take eggs up to her early on a Sunday morning. One New Year's day my mum, who would have been about six years old was awake and up and wanted to go with him – he said 'yes' and off they trotted. Now everyone knows that a six year old can start off walking very happily but as my mother told me, when they got to the bottom of Markham Road she started lagging and her dad walked on. He was at the top of the hill by the time she reached the Fox and Hounds and something odd struck her…

She could hear music. There was drumming and fiddling and she wondered who was still up in the Fox and Hounds so early in the morning making all that music. She didn't like being left behind however and ran up the hill to catch up with her dad.

Later as she walked back down with her father she told him about the music she'd heard on the way up and he gave her a wry smile and said 'you must of heard the ghosts of the minstrels from the church seeing in the New Year'. Here is the ghost story he referred to.

On January 30th 1848 a poster was put up in the village. It read

£10 REWARD

Whereas on the Evening of the 31st December, 1847 or on the Saturday or Sunday morning following, some evil disposed person or persons did maliciously destroy the Organ in the parish church of Wroughton.

The above reward is offered for the apprehension of the offender or offenders, and will be paid by the church wardens of the aforesaid parish on the conviction of the offenders, party or parties.

January
30th
1848

In the previous year, 1847 the vicar had spent a lot of time raising money to modernize and improve the condition of the church building as it had fallen into disrepair. The roof leaked and there was woodworm and damp. The fundraising was a great success and the church was fully refurbished, the old minstrel's gallery was pulled out and a brand new organ installed.

You'd think this was a good thing, however allegedly several Wroughtonians took great exception to the improvements. The reason for this was that the fiddlers, pipers and drummers who had accompanied services for centuries were no longer needed.

Legend has it that the minstrels who had once enjoyed the kudos and no doubt a small payment for playing at religious ceremonies, were very resentful that the minstrel's gallery had been removed and replaced by an organ and an organist. It is said that the minstrels after imbibing a few too many alcoholic beverages that New Year's Eve, entered the church and destroyed the organ. They then returned to the Drum and Monkey to finish off their revels into the New Year. Back in 1847 the Fox and Hounds was simply a cottage that brewed beer and was called The Drum and Monkey.

And where I wonder does that name come from, does it have something to do with that night. Was the drum a reference to the drum that would stop beating at the church and the monkey a reference to the organ, as in organ grinder's monkey? Who knows?

But if you're walking by the old Drum and Monkey in the early morning in the heart of winter and think you can hear a fiddle, pipe and drum…you had better believe your ears. Incidentally, no one was ever apprehended for the destruction of the organ in the parish church.

Other ghosts have also been associated with the Fox and Hounds. Folk history tells of a fire that killed a young girl who now haunts the bar and children have for many years been allegedly heard playing in the corridors of the lodgings at the back of the pub. One story says that a man was checking his reflection in a mirror that hung in the lounge and noticed the reflection of a little girl of 8 or 9 stood behind him. Their eyes met, but when he turned around to give her a grin no one was there.

An ex landlady also told me the story of a little girl that haunted an upstairs laundry room. Possibly the same little girl who haunts the bar. 'The temperature would suddenly drop and we'd know she was there.' The face of a young girl has also been seen in an upstairs window when the pub was empty.

The Paranormal Investigation at the Fox and Hounds

In May 2017 I was invited as an observer to a paranormal investigation at the pub. The investigation was prompted by a variety of disturbances at the premises. Doors were found open when they'd been closed, items had been moved and the sounds of children were heard running and playing. There were also problems with lights turning on and off and light bulbs blowing and beer pumps not functioning.

Here is a brief description of that investigation and my subsequent research. The investigation was led by VIP Paranormal Investigations and attended by Wiltshire Paranormal, myself and the pub manager. The 'Foxes Den' a tastefully decorated dining area, (which was once the outside smoking area) was the base room, where plans for the evening were discussed and a host of various ghost detecting devices were tested and batteries charged to maximum.

The devices included night vision cameras, K2 meters which use broadband pass technology and light up when they detect electro-magnetic energy and live feed microphones. There were also laser grids and rem pods, rem pods detect energy disturbances and fluctuations and use coloured lights and audible tones to alert you to disturbances.

With all this in place we started the investigation by splitting into groups. I accompanied one of the investigators to the hotel rooms which occupy a separate building at the back of the pub. There are six rooms and reports say that children can be heard running down the corridors giggling and playing. A locked off camera was set up at one end of the corridor and a control item, a teddy bear was positioned to record any 'ghost child' that might try to move it. We sat there silently trying not to chat, although the ambient corridor lighting was quite off putting. We had a sound enhancing device.

At the end of the corridor we did think there may have been whispering but that could have been from one of the rooms. I have been told that over the years many guests have complained about children playing in the corridor when no children have actually been there. Outside I was using the sound magnification and distinctly heard running, although so close to the fields it could have been wildlife, but it did make me sit up and take notice.

When we went back inside the pub I noted a lot of the ghost hunting devices I previously mentioned were set up around the bar area. We sat around a table under one of the old beams and questions were thrown into the air by each person around the table. The K2 meters were very active, although when I produced my phone from my pocket to take pictures I was told that some of the activity may have been due to the android WI-FI. The inexplicable moments were when the light grid was activated, the vibration detectors kept going off and the batteries on some of the devices drained with hardly any usage.

There was also some glasswork, an upturned glass was put on the round table, we touched the top lightly with the tips of our fingers and questions were asked. To be honest the table surface wasn't smooth and therefore presented a problem for any ghostly entity with a desire to communicate.

The individual that provided insight as a 'sensitive' thought that there was a Reverent Tom or Rev Tom that had been active on the premises and had a perverted interest in children. Local stories suggest that children from the workhouse in Markham Road may have been working there, and there is evidence to suggest that the children were hired out as cheap labour either to help fund the workhouse or to line the pockets of the work house employees. The 'medium' also picked up on a girl at the top of the stairs who he thought was called Emily. The team had come to the investigation with some historical facts, some hearsay, and some vague details based on what was happening. Sometimes it's hard to untangle them.

They knew that the pub had originally been cottages, at least by 1798. This is true. I began researching the pub myself and looked into the ownership. It was indeed two cottages. One of which was occupied by Luke Curtis who lived there in 1851 as a 'beer-house keeper'. At this time it was known as 'The Drum and Monkey'. On the same premises lived his wife Martha, their 4 children, and his mother in law, Sarah Dunn – who is described as a 'landed proprietor', plus 3 lodgers. Bit of a squash no doubt.

On April 26th 1860 the Wiltshire Independent Newspaper reports a fire at the Curtis' beer house, describing the location exactly and saying that both cottages were consumed by fire, - although no one died as local legend has it. (I would point out this doesn't eliminate a death by fire at some time in the building's past).

Poor Luke wasn't having much luck however as only 2 weeks later on May 7th 1860 the Swindon Advertiser reports that having just moved into a house further up the hill with his 8 children another fire broke out which destroyed many houses and found them homeless once again. (This is the area called the Castle that I pointed out as you were following the ghost walk down the hill and is opposite the bench).

Things must have been restored somewhat by 1861 because we find him back at the beer house with his wife, 8 children and 82 year old mother in law, but no room for lodgers. The two oldest children are now described as servants, probably working locally.

In July 1866 things must have been restored even more as the cottages are up for auction. One described as a beer house and the land considered highly desirable according to the Swindon Advertiser. It seems that only one cottage is sold as Luke Curtis is still at the location in 1871 with his wife and their 4 youngest children. He is 53. He is now described as an agricultural labourer, no beer house is mentioned – and still living there in 1881 he's described as a general labourer and by then only 2 children live at home with him and Martha his wife.

I couldn't make the 'Emily' connection with Luke and his family. The children were called Matilda, Caroline, Martha, Frederick, Richard, Charles, George, Maria, Henry, Eliza and Joseph. Of course that doesn't exclude an Emily from living there at any other time.

So what happened to Luke Curtis? Well the Swindon Advertiser can enlighten us as on 22nd January 1887 both cottages are up for auction again.

Here is the piece from the paper…

'Lot 1 – semi-detached free hold dwelling house containing sitting room, kitchen, wash-house, three bedrooms and usual offices, with the gardens adjoining such dwelling house. All which premises are known as No.1 Queensland Villas, Workhouse Road, Wroughton and are in the occupation of Mrs. Lucy Jane Norton.

Lot 2. Semi-detached free hold dwelling house adjoining Lot 1 and containing sitting room, kitchen, three bedrooms and usual offices with the garden adjoining such dwelling house all which premises are known as No 2 Queensland Villas, Workhouse Road, Wroughton and are in the occupation of Mr. Luke Curtis.'

I would just add that Mr. Curtis appears in the local press of the time quite frequently, but it's not as you might suspect for some nefarious beer house brawling. It's for his prize onions!

The ghost hunt findings were inconclusive. Yes, there were inexplicable responses from the equipment and the light show was typical of children's playful behavior – but I wasn't convinced. That so many children grew up at the cottages and so many individuals spent time at the beer house would suggest some kind of energy still associated with the place but nothing specific came out of the investigation.
Now if you've finished your beverage let's move on.

High Street, Wroughton in 1913. On the right side of the street is the business premises of Blacksmith and Farrier John Rudman, the front of the Primitive Methodist chapel (the Church Institute) can just be seen next door, a little further back from the road

Rudman's Forge

From the Fox and Hounds go down the hill a little and look across the road. At the side of The Oxhouse which is now someone's garage was the business premises of Blacksmith and Farrier John Rudman for farm animals (see picture on p. 28) and next to this is…

The Church Institute

What you're seeing is two houses but it was originally built as the Primitive Methodist chapel in 1853. On Sunday afternoons during the 1st World War a lady called Miss Chandler who lived in Markham Cottages organised volunteers here. They would supply tea and bake cakes and serve them here, at the Church Institute for soldiers who would come down from Chiseldon Camp. There was always a queue as it was very popular. There's a story associated with this building, about a young man coming to meet his friend here…but we'll save it till we get down to the Co-op.

A lady who once lived in one of the two houses that once comprised the Primitive Methodist chapel told me about a time she was in one of the back bedrooms looking out over the woods. Suddenly she began hearing voices as if it someone was in the bedroom with her. She wasn't frightened, just curious.

Coloured orbs have also been seen in the area outside of the Methodist Chapel/Church Institute. Orbs are supposed to be a sign of paranormal activity. Are they the ghosts of those young men hoping for a cuppa and the camaraderie of their peers all those years ago? Or are they the drunken, half seen hallucinations of someone who has had one too many in the Carter's Rest which is where we will stop next.

The Carter's Rest, 1995 with landlord Andy and his wife Sue

The Carter's Rest

The Carter's Rest looks very Victorian with its gable ends however this building work was actually done in 1912. Prior to this the pub looked more like a residential dwelling than a public house.

There are two ghost stories associated with The Carter's Rest with some additional curiosities which have no real explanation. The first relates to a ghost dog, often seen as a dark Labrador size dog. Twenty years or so ago, the landlord was a chap called Andy (see picture on the opposite page), and he would often tell customers about the resident ghost dog. His personal experience was almost tripping over a dog behind the bar while he was serving a couple of pints. He put the drinks on the bar and looked round with surprise as he didn't have a dog. There was no dog to be found.

The story of the dog is quite common. I know people who have seen the dog and sometimes if you're sat at a table, especially in the lounge, you may think a dog is leaning against your legs but when you take a look, nothing is there.

One of those curiosities which doesn't immediately suggest a ghost but has an unsettling effect are lights flickering towards the back of the Lounge bar by the toilets. They dim and then come back on. Is that an electrical fault or a power surge? I suppose it could be explained in lots of ways – but again this is a phenomenon that many have experienced.

The ghost story that stands out is about two framed photographs which still hang in the pub. These were given to the Carter's Rest by the local history group when Andy, (who almost tripped over the ghost dog), was the manager. On the next page is one of the pictures and at the feet of the man in shirt sleeves you can see a dog.

One of the pictures that still hangs on the wall of the Carter's Rest

The land lord was really pleased with his two pictures and hung them on the wall in the bar. That night he went to bed but when he got up in the morning the pictures were both on the floor. They were face down and the glass in each frame was intact but he found them on the other side of the room as if someone had thrown them across the bar.

Andy was a bit spooked but decided to give it another go so he rehung them. That night he went to bed as normal checking that they were still in place before he went. Everything was as usual, nothing was out of place. But, when he got up in the morning he found them again on the other side of the room, face down, unbroken. Not one to push his luck he hung them in the lounge and the next day although he went downstairs with a little trepidation they were still hung up and they stayed hung in the same place until this year 2019.

Today after a very tasteful refurbishment I notice that both pictures have been rehung and one of them has made it into the bar. A chat with the landlady revealed that nothing spooky has happened and the pictures have not been found on the floor at any time.

I wondered if after all these years the ghosts of the past have made peace with the decor of the present and now find the bar a perfectly presentable place to hang. I have been informed however that it was a particular place in the bar that caused the problem. It remains to be seen that if the photographs were hung in the place that Andy originally hung them in the bar – if they would again be found on the floor on the other side of the room, face down, but intact.

As a matter of interest the very same supernatural incident occurred many years ago in a thatched cottage in Greens Lane owned at the time by Pete and Freda Patterson. I would be interested to hear of any similar stories that have been experienced in the village.

Looking East down the High Street circa 1910

Looking West up the High Street circa 1920 with The Carter's Rest recognizable in the middle of the photograph. Number 59 High Street, the subject of my next ghost story is a couple of doors down with a gabled porch.

59 High Street

This double fronted Victorian house was originally the second house down from The Carter's Rest. The house between the pub and 59 High Street was knocked down in the 1970's to access the pub car park at the back. Richard and Sarah currently live here and have done so for a number of years. However they do not live alone.

Richard found out some spooky stories associated with the house and related them to me prior to telling me about his own ghostly experiences. He was told that when a plumber was doing some work in the kitchen he inexplicably ran out of the house and refused to go back in. Apparently someone had to retrieve his tools. Another time a decorator was painting one of the upstairs rooms when the bedroom door closed and he was unable to open it. Eventually it opened and he found his stock of paint ruined as the lids of the tins had shot off and the tins had buckled.

The third story relates to a previous resident having a visit from her son and granddaughter. The granddaughter disappeared upstairs and she could be heard talking to someone. When she came down they asked her what she was doing and she said, 'talking to the old lady in the bed'.

Having lived in the house for some time now Richard says they're used to the strange going's on, although he does remain cautious and was reluctant to let me go in the house as he felt the 'ghost' might not like it. They often experience items being moved or going missing for several days. Most recently their passports which were left on the second step of the stairs disappeared for two days. They were eventually found upstairs under a statue, with just a little bit of passport peeping out. Ornamental birds hanging from the ceiling are often found on the other side of the room and they've experienced electrical circuits cutting out and the TV and radio turning on and off.

Richard's most frightening experience was when Sarah was away for the night. He was watching TV and felt that he wasn't alone. He was sitting on the leather sofa and felt something beside him and saw the sofa flatten as if something or someone had sat next to him. Still reeling from what was happening he then saw a dark shadow pass in front of the fire.

Can this phenomena be explained by anything other than a ghost? Is it the old lady that the child thought she was talking to in the bedroom? Before moving into the house Richard didn't believe in ghosts. He does now. Do you?

The White Hart circa 1930 the subject of our next ghost story. The tenant at the time of this photograph was David Long who pulled pints there from 1923 to 1939

The White Hart

The White Hart is a little further down the hill on the other side of the road. You can't fail to notice this very picturesque and olde worlde thatched inn.

A hart is the archaic name for a stag and if you live around Wroughton, although you may not have seen a stag you're likely to have seen a lot of deer. The name of the pub also echoes Wroughton's origins. Was the name an acknowledgement of Ella the horned Goddess? Or even Herne the antlered God of the pagans. In ancient times a white hart was particularly lucky and at a time when hunting was a common pastime a white hart was to be avoided at all costs as killing one would bring an abundance of bad luck.

The pub was probably an Inn around 300 years ago, but an earlier building is likely to have stood here. Luckily it wasn't destroyed by either the 1860 Castle fire or the 1896 great fire that ravaged part of the High Street, especially given its thatched roof. In Victorian times up until the early 1900's the front yard was a smithy for local tradesman's horses. I cannot find out when it first took the name White Hart, there's no previous name that I know of. The White Hart as well as being the 5th most popular pub name in Britain is also one used since the 12th century, when folk memory and ancient traditions were still strong.

I worked here in the early 1990's for Adrian Potts who later went on to run The Barge at Honey Street. They didn't know much about the history, but his wife told me she would never go up the 2nd flight of stairs where you see the little window at the side, (see picture on p.38) by herself as she always thought she was being watched. This feeling of 'being watched' has been told to me by someone else who worked at the pub in the early years of the 21st century.

The ghost that haunts The White Hart is allegedly that of an old woman. She's been seen on numerous occasions either walking from the skittle alley to the fireplace or actually sat in the fireplace knitting, crocheting or sewing. Apparently she wears a little white bonnet, white collar and cuffs and a long skirt. This was the dress of most women for several hundred years, if not longer so it would be hard to pin point where in history the lady of the White Hart comes from.

The White Hart, the window under the gable of the near chimney, lights the staircase which is believed to be haunted

The sweet shop

Further down the High Street on the same side as the Carter's Rest we come to School Lane. Here just behind us is the house where once lived Richard Austen with his daughter, who sold sweets on the premises. The Swindon poet Alfred Williams, gathered together scenes of rural Victorian life and he wrote about Dicky Austen in 1913 in his writings 'In a Wiltshire Village'. This is what he says

'At Wroughton, 'Dicky' Austin, the old church clerk, nearly ninety years of age, lives in a small cottage halfway down the hill, together with a middle aged daughter, who tends him in his infirmity. He is tall and upright, silver haired, with large kind eyes, prominent nose and thin side-beard, but his old hand trembles and his head shakes visibly.'

I'd thoroughly recommend a complete read of Alfred Williams to give you a real insight into life in the village and the villages of Wiltshire at this time.

The sweet shop circa 1920, the railings to school lane can just be seen on the right of the elderly gentleman

Here you can see the second cottage from Sun Lane corner on the right of the picture where the next ghost story unfolds

The second cottage from Sun Lane corner

This cottage has been changed around a lot over the years and some parts can probably be dated to Elizabethan times, maybe earlier. When decorating in a dark corner the lady who lives here found some odd shaped wooden cones in the ceiling beam, which she later discovered were reed burners. A poor family without access to candles would have burnt reeds collected from the river at the bottom of the lane for light.

The owner of this house told me that when she first moved into the cottage, the first thing she noticed was a strong floral scent in the attic which comes and goes. Another story she related was that when her children were young they would say that after being put to bed they could hear the rustle of a dress around their beds as if someone was checking on them. Thinking it was their mum they told her to stop doing it as she was waking them up….she didn't tell them that it wasn't her!

This story has been corroborated from another source. I was watching the carnival procession coming down the High Street one year and an old lady came up to me and asked me if I did the ghost walks. When I nodded she pointed at this very same house and said, 'I can tell you about a ghost in that house.' She continued by saying that when she was a little girl she stayed with a relative in the house and she would hide under the blankets when she went to bed as a ghost would walk around her bed at night.

Another ghost that's been seen at this cottage is the spectre of a well-dressed man from another age. He wears a waist coat over a white shirt, tweed jacket and gaiters and a hat that's described as like a trilby but smaller. He appears in the corner of the room and walks out of what was once the back door, but is now an internal door.

He always appears at autumn and through winter. It's as if he's going through the motions like a video clip that's trapped in time.

A medium who visited the cottage said the man was going to the house next door. The house next door was for a long time the butcher's shop and was particularly well known for its smoked bacon. The cottage very oddly has a fireplace at each end of the living space – one room with two fire places is very unusual, and while refurbishing the owner found a meat hook hanging from the ceiling in the area where the ghostly figure is seen.

Who is this well-dressed man? With no apron he's not likely to be the butcher, is he checking his smoked hams hanging from the beams? Could he be a spirit or an image imprinted on the atmosphere? Make up your own minds!

Now take the track on your right that leads down Sun Lane, walk a couple of hundred yards and look at the house that faces onto the lane. This was once the public house called The Rising Sun.

The Rising Sun circa 1908

The Rising Sun

The Rising Sun was a public house along Sun Lane, owned and run by the Hawkins family. Cecil Hawkins who was a popular figure in the village up until his death some 25 years ago maintained that a building had stood here in the 1660's. It originally had a thatch which was singed during the great fire of Wroughton, (which started in Sun Lane), and was later replaced by slate tiles. You will also see that some of the windows are blocked up, this is because in the reign of George III there was a window tax of 6d per window which the owner at the time refused to pay.

The current owners found lots of bits and pieces when they renovated the house harking back to when the building was a public house. Among their finds were a hoard of clay pipes stuffed into a cubby hole in the ceiling in the bar, playing cards, a hat pin, coins and even a packet of woodbines.

The pub didn't get its license renewed in 1909, and some say it's because a lot of wheeling and dealing around poached merchandise took place and the local magistrates were hoping to stop it by denying the license. The official reason given by the magistrates was that Wroughton had too many pubs!

The lady who now lives here told me that one day she was chatting with a friend in the living room, (the living room used to be the men's bar). Her friend's husband was sat watching the cricket on the TV when he looked over at them and shivered. He took a deep breath and said.
'There's been a lot of people in here'.
The owner told him that he was sat in the bar of what was a pub over a century ago, and there was once always a lot of people there.
'Yes,' he said, 'I can feel them…'

Given that it was once a busy public house the cottage has a very peaceful atmosphere. I spent time talking to Cecil Hawkins sat in the front room where the window fronts Sun Lane. Cecil had been brought up living in the pub and he and my grandfather both served in the Home Guard in Wroughton during the 2nd World War.

As an old man Cecil lived in the High Street, but every day he came and dug over the garden behind the Sun Inn and when the digging became too hard he'd light a fire and sit in the front room and while away his days remembering the good times past. He was a lovely old chap.

As you continue to walk down Sun Lane you will see some brick outhouses in the garden to your right, close to the house. These were once used to brew beer. At the end of the garden there is a well which is no longer in use.

Sun Lane was called Sun Lane as it was a sun trap that enjoyed the full heat of the day's sun.

Home Guard photograph circa 1941. Cecil Hawkins standing back row right, my grandfather, Archie Page seated front left

The Pest House and the Great Fire of Wroughton

If you had been walking down Sun Lane on 29th July 1896 you would have met quite a commotion as this is where the Great Fire of Wroughton began in a hay rick at King's Farm. The fire spread quickly and before long 5 hay ricks were ablaze and the thatches of nearby cottages, which once stood in the vicinity of The Co-op. Before I tell you more about The Great Fire of Wroughton however you need to proceed along Sun Lane and continue until you reach the stream where another Wroughton ghost is said to be seen.

Up until around 1851 Sun Lane would have led you to the Pest House. In other words the Pestilence house. In times gone by diseases which we're now vaccinated for, like whooping cough, measles and mumps had a very low recovery rate, but additionally there were other dreaded diseases that are no longer common to the UK, like small pox, cholera and the dreaded 'fever'. They were all very contagious and caused many deaths in the villages of England and Wroughton was no exception. The house of pestilence saw the demise of many Wroughtonians.

There's still a small ridge on the hill, although covered with new trees, quite close to the fence line at the top which shows where the Pest House once stood. No one was allowed to visit the pest house and provisions were left on the village side of the stream to be collected. In fact a special right of way was made from the Pest House to the stream so that there was no fear of accidentally meeting someone that was going to or from the Pest House.

Eventually as there was less need for a house of Pestilence it fell out of use and another house was built and lived in by the Gray family from 1851. They were thatcher's, a very traditional trade and lived there for the following 50 years into the 20th Century.

When you reach the stream I ask you to think back to that time when this was the crossing where Wroughton people would bring their loved ones who were suffering from cholera or small pox. This is where they would say good bye and watch as their family member crossed the stream and headed to the Pest House hoping for recovery, praying for a miracle.

It's at this small bridge a man has been seen waiting. He's wearing dark clothes and has dark hair and when seen he's been mistaken for a living person waiting by the stream. I was told about him by a local man who's no longer alive and the last sighting was back in the 80's a long time before the new houses you see behind you were built. If you have seen him in recent times I would be interested in hearing about your experience.

He waits here patiently until someone talks to him or stares at him and then he will disappear before your eyes. Who could this man be and what is he doing here? When investigating this phenomenon a ghostly candidate did surface. I tentatively suggest that the spectre is that of Mr. King who actually owned the land on which the Pest House stood and gives his name to the present wood that stands on the same land.

In 1784 there was a smallpox epidemic in Wroughton and the Parish Register lists four members of his family, two young women and two tiny children all dying in the epidemic that year. Could it be that he waits here for news? News that impacted him so much that his ghost still haunts this place? Does Mr. King still wait and hope for better news?

*Here is a picture of Wroughton from the Andrews' and Dury's Map of Wiltshire
1773 I have identified the Pest House with a dot between
the H and T of Wroughton*

Now make your way back to the main road via the path that takes you
to the Co-op. As you reach the car park at the back of the Co-op bring
your thoughts back to that hot summer of the 1896 fire of Wroughton.
The thatches of the cottages here are all ablaze and the woman are
trying to rescue their belongings from their burning homes. There is no
modern fire engine to come and douse the flames and no water
hydrants, only adrenalin and human perseverance. To make matters
worse a summer breeze is blowing sparks to nearby thatches. Imagine
the panic and fear that gripped everyone.

The Wroughton History book 2 gives a gripping account of the fire
and I would refer you to that to find out more. But isn't it interesting
and moving to know that you are walking where this fascinating piece
of Wroughton social history occurred?

This picture shows the devastation caused by the 1896 Great Fire of Wroughton. This is the area where the Co-op now stands

The ghost on the wall

As you walk past the back car park of the Co-op there's a wall and it was only recently that someone wrote to me about an apparition seen at this location. The lady said her husband saw a ghost sitting on this wall when he was coming home about 1.30am. The lady wrote 'My husband came home at 1.30 this morning properly spooked by an apparition laughing at him, it's still unnerved him this morning. He's normally rational and never really believed in this sort of thing before.'

It didn't sound like the spirit by the stream, which has a somber appearance. However there is a theory given at the time of the Great fire of Wroughton that the fire was started by boys playing with matches. The Sun Lane hay ricks extended towards what would now be the back car park of the Co-op. Maybe the dark, laughing apparition is malicious, maybe a prankster but the fire was real and the apparition of the man laughing on the wall may be the person that started that fire.

Another story that comes to mind is the story of the 'pig on the wall'. Many years ago a Wroughton resident had purchased his piglet and was taking it home in a sack. As he came on to the High Street the band was passing by and he put his pig on the wall in the sack while he stopped to enjoy the music. Apparently though this was by the Church Hall and not where the Co-op now stands

If anyone else has had any unusual experiences that might flesh out the story of the apparition laughing on the wall of the Co-op car park please let me know.

How many pictures of unknown soldiers sit in a box of postcards in junk shops around the country? The faces of young men stare into the camera, a captured memory for those left behind. Our next ghost story is about one such soldier

An unknown soldier

The Soldier Boy

When you reach the main road position yourself safely on the pavement so that you can look down Wharf Road. It's a fast road now but sometimes you see people walking or running down Wharf Road between the Elcombe and Mill Lane turning, (which is the turn off to Waitrose now). If you are driving that way by any chance and see a young man walking that route make a mental note of what he's wearing. Stories tell of people driving down this road and stopping to offer a lift to a lad in uniform. When they turn round to let him in the car, he's mysteriously disappeared. This is one of those generic ghost stories that is told all over the world with slightly different descriptions, but the pattern is always the same. Someone needs a lift, the car stops but there's no one there. However, there is a local story that lends itself to this mysterious tale.

Apparently during the First World War a lad from Lydiard met a pal in France and they promised to meet up when they were back home at Miss Chandler's Sunday tea and cake for serviceman. The story goes that the boy from Lydiard never made it back from the front but his spirit is still trying to meet up with his pal. Probably farm lads serving together in the Wiltshire Regiment. If you drive this road, be sure to notice any walkers and what they are wearing.

A lady on one of my ghost walks told me that she drove to pick her teenage son up from a party about 11.30 at night. As she drove along Wharf Road between the Elcombe turning and Mill Lane, she saw a man, looking quite bedraggled and dressed oddly, though she couldn't quite put her finger on why he caught her attention. It worried her and when she got home and told her husband, they both went out to try to find him. After stopping the car and searching up and down the road (she thought he may have fallen in the ditch) they found no one.

The original Ely Inn 1907. The building at this time lay back from the road and the Tibbles family were in residence.

From the Co-op to the Ely

As you walk down the High Street to what was once a pub called the Ely Inn you will pass an area that would have been devastated by the 1896 fire. It was chance that kept the pub from being burnt to the ground. When the fire reached the Ely the wind changed and the Ely was saved from catastrophe.

The Ely, which is now flats but was once a popular inn was named after a famous racehorse. The Ely in its present form was rebuilt in 1914, but a pub has stood in this area for several hundred years. The previous name of the pub was The Cooper's Arms which brewed beer on the premises. The grounds here were huge and the fields at the back were a playground for local children well into the 20th Century.
If you're reading this and you know any ghost stories about this pub or area or have experienced anything unexplainable please let me know.

The new Ely Inn, post war picture, built closer to the road

Fairwater House and adjoining stables were built approximately 1700. Horse racing played a major role in Wroughton's history.

Positioned side-on to the High Street

Fairwater House

I was told this story when I'd just moved back to the village with my parents in the mid 1970's. A friend came to stay the night and being summer we went for a walk. Although we were under 18 we slipped into the Ely and feeling very daring ordered two halves of cider and were chuffed to bits when the barmaid served us without batting an eyelid. We were sat by a window and there was an old chap near us pondering his pint of beer and puffing away on a pipe that kept going out.

Tricia, my friend and I were talking about horror films, (I think we'd seen The Omen a few weeks before) and the old boy jumped into our conversation and said he had a story about ghost hounds. I think we were in fits of giggles at the time but the story stayed with me.

The old man said that there were ghost dogs in Fairwater House and that they howled when there was trouble. I've never heard this story since and would be interested if anyone else knows anything about it. I began looking into the history of Fairwater House and as always Wroughton History books provided pertinent information, which may or may not be relevant to the ghost dog story the old chap told us in the Ely, but this history seems to fit around the ghost story. You must make up your own minds.

The tale begins in the 1920's when a Mr. Matheson resided at Fairwater House. Mr. Matheson had been a solicitor but when he lost his sight he retired to breed whippets and terriers. He was well liked in the village and had a good reputation.

Another man, an entrepreneur called Mr. Hartell rented some of the stables at Fairwater House from Mr. Matheson for his race horses. Unlike Mr. Matheson, Mr. Hartell had a poor reputation. Allegedly he mistreated his jockeys and didn't pay his bills and local people disliked him.

One story says that Mr. Hartell attacked Mr. Matheson and that they had a dispute where Hartell began breaking windows at Fairwater house. This disturbed Mr. Matheson's whippets and terriers who began barking and howling. When local people heard the racket they came to Mr. Matheson's aid and soon after that Mr. Hartell left Wroughton, was declared bankrupt – and never seen again.

So are the howling hounds based on this particular story or is there another I'm yet to hear? I've occasionally walked past a random house and heard a howling dog within. It's not an unusual occurrence. Some dogs do howl when their owners leave them alone in the house. Is a lonely dog the real source of the story of the hounds (or should we say whippets) of Fairwater House?

A post note to this story is that on one of the walks a lady came up to me after I told this story and said, - 'Mr. Matheson is so glad you told his story. He's been stood at your side nodding and smiling for the last five minutes'. It did send a shiver down my spine and suggests Mr. Matheson liked Fairwater House so much he never left.

Here with his beloved hounds Mr. Matheson is pictured 2ⁿᵈ from the left. Close inspection reveals he wears dark lenses in his glasses

Spencer's Farm and the High Street

Across the Road we can see Spencer's Farm and until about 30 years ago an old barn dating from the 1600's stood in the grounds. In the 19th Century the Farm was called Zoar Marsh Farm and was owned by the Buckland family, the name was changed to Spencer's Farm in the early 20th Century and was then owned by Teddy Hawkins. Teddy owned a transport business known as The Old Firm. The sound of bus engines running when there's no bus to be seen are still said to be heard if you happen to be walking down the High Street late at night.

People have also said they've seen buses from times past travelling up and down the High Street. This might be because of the close proximity to The Science Museum and the type of vehicle events that are sometimes held there. Or maybe 'The Old Firm's' ghostly buses are still picking up their spirit passengers.

It's not only the sound of ghostly buses that can be heard in the High Street, the sound of disembodied horse's hooves have also been reported. The village has a rich history of race horse training and the sound of horses being taken by jockeys through the village to the gallops was once very common. Is it surprising that their ghostly hooves can still be heard?

It's also been suggested that the ghostly sounds of horses trotting through the village are those of Oliver Cromwell's New Model Army coming down the High Street heading towards Oxford during the Civil War (1642 to 1651). It was said that the Yew Hedge around Ivery House was planted to commemorate this and was taught as fact to school children in the village up until the 1900's.

There doesn't seem to be any evidence that Cromwell travelled through Wroughton, so if it's not Cromwell's horses then it seems likely that the hooves that are heard are the hooves of the many horses that were trained in Wroughton. Wroughton was once one of the leading race horse training locations in England.

An interesting foot note to this is that in 1998 a hoard of coins was found buried in the garden of Waterfall Cottage in the Pitchens and the coins all date up to, but not after 1643 – and most of the coins are Royalist coins. These would probably have been paid to the miller who was selling bread to the Royalists. Oddly enough John and Bartholomew Brind who lived at the cottage at the time, remained alive throughout the conflict and it is curious that they didn't dig up their hoard of coins in the time after the civil war.

Could it be that a hedge was planted and called The Oliver Cromwell Hedge to hide the fact that villagers did very well out of the Royalists and did a lot of trade with them? The last thing they wanted was for the Roundheads to think they had Royalist leanings once the Roundheads came to power. John and Bartholomew probably thought the same and may have left the hoard buried waiting for a safer time to unearth it. That safer time never came. We'll never know the truth - so all I can say is listen out for those ghostly hooves in the High Street.

The Oliver Cromwell Hedge

The River Ray

As we walk towards the Three Horse Shoes, which is now called The Brown Jack, follow the path between the stream and the original road down to Mill brook. Here the overflow from the reservoir at Overtown merges with the stream from Markham Bottom to form the Wroughton Brook, which further on becomes the River Ray. This takes our story back to the Battle of Ellendun which I referred to at the beginning of this booklet.

The chroniclers tell us that after the battle the River Ray ran red with the blood of the slain. It was the decisive battle of Anglo Saxons against Mercians. It's said that on the downs you can still hear the clash of sword against sword.

There are several other interesting stories you can consider as you walk over to the Brown Jack for a pint of beer or glass of wine. Prior's Hill that climbs slowly towards the downs on your right has a natural spring about half way up that trickles from the left side of the road as you ascend.

Local children used to call the water from the spring 'witch's water' and were warned not to drink it or go near it. As a little girl, a local resident explained that she would walk to the other side of the road rather than even get near the witch's water.

When the water was eventually tested in the 20th Century by the Highworth Rural and District Medical officer it was pronounced unfit for drinking and piped water was installed.

Deer shedding velvet as antlers grow

The Headless Horseman

No village ghost story is complete without a tale about a headless horseman and Wroughton is no different. Several hundred years ago it was said that a headless horseman rode from Marlborough across the downs to Wroughton on the night of the full moon and anyone who saw it would be cursed. Now that might sound rather over the top in this day and age but in those days people were very susceptible to superstition – life was very often hand to mouth and no one wanted to tip the balance of fate on purpose.

Well was there a headless horseman? Our best guess is that given the number of pubs in the area, the full moon was a good time to move contraband and in order to deter the local populace from being out and about (given that poaching was a large part of village life) a frightening headless horseman was invented.

There is another suggestion…which ties in nicely with Ellen of the Ways the antler Goddess who may have given her name to our village. A stag's new antlers have a velvety coating which is shed and looks like bloody, torn fabric. When the velvet is being shed the stag will often rub it's antlers on the bark of trees and sometimes undergrowth becomes tangled in the antlers as well. In fact the velvet and tangled ivy vines might well look like a cloak. A poor farm hand out on the downs in the twilight might well have thought a perfectly normal phenomenon was something supernatural. Which theory do you prefer?

The Three Horseshoes, the name was changed to The Brown Jack in 1947 to honour the village's favourite race horse

The Brown Jack skittle alley (below) is believed to be 400 years old

The Brown Jack

The Brown Jack public house in Priors Hill

And so we arrive at the Brown Jack, the end of the Ghost Walk.

The current pub was built in 1901 after the original thatched roofed pub burnt down. The skittle alley survived the fire and may be around 300 to 400 years old which gives an indication of the age of the original building. The pub grounds were once extensive until houses were built on the land and the carpark was laid. It was originally called the Three Horseshoes.

The previous landlady told me that she was convinced that the ghost of a tall man haunted the pub. She affectionately named him George and the name has stuck. She thought that he once lived in a nearby cottage and died in a fire, maybe folk memory of the 1901 fire has fueled this suspicion, although I can't find any solid evidence of deaths to support this.

George is believed to have set off the motion sensor on a number of occasions in the middle of the night causing the landlady to get the sensor checked by the firm that installed it. It was found to be working perfectly and yet the sensor still continued to go off. The landlady also mentioned that her dog would often sit and stare into a corner of the pub. Most compelling however was when a visiting pool team came to the pub. One member of the team was so sure that someone was leaning over him when he was taking a shot that he abandoned the match altogether.

The pub is now under new management and they have told me that they have not experienced any unusual or supernatural activity. Did the ghost leave with the last publican or is he still there?

Brown Jack, 6 times winner of the Queen Alexandra Stakes.
Ridden by Steve Donoghue

Postscript

I hope you have found these ghostly stories interesting. They are from
the mouths of villagers and visitors who have told me their
supernatural tales and entrusted me with their strangest experiences.
During the course of my ghost walks and because of my interest in the
supernatural tales of the village of Wroughton I am often told stories
about the past inhabitants of this village, from the crying child in the
fields of North Wroughton, to the face in the wall of the cottage in
what the estate agents like to call 'the old quarter'. If you have a strange
or ghostly tale to tell please let me know.
Until next time, - sleep tight.

My family home in 1930 in Perrys Lane, Wroughton

Printed in Great Britain
by Amazon

33952701R00040